BLESSED BY
THE GRACE OF
GOD

What life is about is putting others before yourself.

BLESSED BY THE GRACE OF GOD

What life is about is putting others before yourself.

MICHAEL ALLAN SIVERTSEN

ARPress
ILLUMINATING IDEAS
EMPOWERING VOICES

ARPress
45 Dan Road Suite 5
Canton MA 02021

Hotline: 1(888) 821-0229
Fax: 1(508) 545-7580

Ordering Information:

Quantity sales. Special discounts are available on quantity purchases by corporations, associations, and others. For details, contact the publisher at the address above.

Printed in the United States of America.

ISBN-13:   Paperback   979-8-89330-370-4

               eBook   979-8-89330-371-1

Library of Congress Control Number: 2024900758

Table Of Contents

DEDICATION

I dedicate this book to God, who will always love us more than we will ever know.

INTRODUCTION

I've always loved the Lord, but I didn't always follow the path he wanted me to. I lived by my own motto. A man has to do, what a man has to do, when a man has to do it. I was too blind to realize that God wants us to embrace a life full of peace and happiness.

I've experienced more things in my life than one hundred people put together. Good and bad things would always occur. Unbelievable and mind-boggling experiences. If I had given more devotion to God a lot of my troubles could have been avoided.

God is a jealous God and demands our loyalty, twenty-four hours and seven days a week. Through all my trials and tribulations, God never abandoned me. He lets us make our own mistakes, and in his eyes, he sees everything. God would always protect me, whether I did good or bad. God is my best friend. He has been beside me all of my life.

I know God personally. I've always loved our Lord, but I never lived the way that he wanted me to. He let me make my own mistakes. We are supposed to learn from our mistakes. One thing I realize is, if I didn't have God in my life, how would I learn?

I was a bad boy when I was younger and that is why bad things would always happen to me. I didn't give God the devotion and praise he deserved. God has been patient with me. For over sixty years I've faithfully prayed. Even though I believe that I disappointed him many times, God has always for gave me.

I have been blessed more than I will ever know. I had to go through hell before I arrived where I am now. I am blessed by the Grace of God. God has shown me the way and shown a lot of patience with me. Actually, I believe that he had to spend a little extra time with me.

Chapter One

Left in a laundry basket at a gas station

I was six months old and my brother was a year and a half when our mother put us in a laundry basket and left us at a gas station. She called my father and said she was leaving. My father couldn't take care of us, so he brought us to our great-aunt and uncle to care for us. They owned and operated a resort in the Northwoods.

It is hard to try to explain the hurt inside when someone doesn't want you, especially a parent. Growing up I never missed my real mother. My great-aunt was the only Mom that I knew or wanted. My great-uncle died when I was six years old. My great-aunt was a strict Christian woman and she gave me some of the best years of my life.

When I got out of line, which could be often I would get whipped with a switch. My lower back had whip marks on it for twenty years. It hurt but, I never cried.

I loved my mom and I knew when I got whipped, I had it coming. Since my great-uncle died, I had to work at an early age. I chopped and split fire wood when I was seven as we had to heat our lodge. I used an electric lawnmower with a hundred-foot cord to mow the grass. We had four cabins and the cord reached all the way. Cutting the grass was a chore. It would take a few hours.

We were young and never complained. We just did the chores and when we were done, we were allowed to do what ever we wanted. I had the best life growing up. I could fish all day and most of the time, I did. In the fifties, fishing was fantastic. We always used worms as they were free. Within minutes I would have five or six pan fish. My mom always cleaned the fish. Most of the time I fished by myself. I had my own boat and motor when I was seven. I lived on a chain of five lakes. I knew where all the good fishing spots were for different fish. I knew a lot of good spots to catch muskies. There is no excitement like it. Once you are hooked, you are hooked. If I wasn't fishing, I would go water skiing. That was almost every day. I had an adventurous life.

We had a Black Lab and if we didn't keep her in the house, she would swim half way across the lake where we were fishing. There was a girls and boys camp on another lake and one or twice a week they would buy soda and candy from us.

There was another resort close to ours so I would take the path through the woods and play baseball or other games with the tourist's children. There were always many ways to have fun. At night some of the other resorts would have Pow Wows and some of the tourists would take me there. I was always fascinated by them. I must have seen a dozen or so. For a young kid, it was very entertaining. Sometimes the tourists would even take me out to dinner with their children.

Living on the resort was always fun, I had different girlfriends that I would see year after year. I was seven when I got my first kiss. I was in second grade. I still remember it like it was yesterday. Her name was Sally Sheldon. She was cute. I opened the closet door and there she was. I kissed her behind the door. A year later she moved away. That was only girlfriend I had in grade school.

Life was an adventure and I wouldn't trade all the good times for anything in the world. I did have a girlfriend that was from Illinois, her family came to our resort for six years in a row. Living on a resort, I developed a lot of friendships.

In the fifties and sixties, people were genuine, and trust was never an issue. People cared more about their fellow man back then. Everything was not about money. That is when people still had values. Everyone treated each other with respect. I sure miss those days.

My Mom always told me, if you don't have nothing nice to say about someone, then don't say nothing at all. She was a smart woman. I have been blessed my entire life and I just didn't realize it.

It was a blessing that my real mother left me in that basket. If that had not happened, I would not have had such a wonderful life. I would not have gotten to know the Lord like I do. I had the best life growing up and it was always surrounded by family and love.

Once I was grown, I learned that my real mother owned a bar and was an alcoholic. She did the right thing by giving me up. It all worked out. I also learned that she was with child when she left and that I had a sister named Debbie that I knew nothing about. There is a reason why things happen the way they do. It is not for us to figure out. We just have to accept that things happen for our own good.

Chapter Two
Won first prize

My great-aunt was an artist. She painted many oil paintings, beautiful works. She was blessed with a talent that was unbelievable. She would sell a lot of her works. She was good. She belonged to the Jack Pine Artist Association.

Everyday when I got home from school, I would watch the Ranger Dan Show. One day they were advertising a drawing contest. You had to draw a lumberjack or paint one and your parents could help you. First prize was a brand new twenty-six-inch bicycle. My mom helped me. She helped me do such a fine job, I just knew I was going to win. I was eleven years old at the time. I told my class mates to watch tv the night they were to announce the winner of the contest because I was going to win. I don't think that anyone believed me, but I won first prize. Back then, this bike was expensive. I was told about sixty bucks. Second place was a set of encyclopedias and third place was two pair of Levi's. When my bike arrived my Uncle, helped me put it together. It was the first bike that I ever owned, and I had to learn how to ride. I took the bike to the top of a hill, got on it and down the hill I went. I was riding by the time I reached the bottom of the hill. That is where I learned to keep my balance. I was so proud of that bike. That was the only bike that ever had. I would ride that bike six miles away to a friend's house. As long as I told my mom where I was going to be, I pretty much did what I wanted.

The first week I had my bike, I probably put on fifty miles. I would ride back and forth on the dirt roads. We lived ten miles from town. I didn't get to town too often. It was a treat when we did. Back when life was simple, and no one worried about what someone else was doing.

Every Spring, I had to help paint our wooden boats. That is probably why I am a house painter today. I was being taught how to paint at an early age. We worked hard and we had fun doing it. I have always enjoyed painting outdoors. To me I have the best work place. Most of the houses that I paint are on a lake. Some of the people that I have painted for still let me fish on their pier by the lake. Where I currently live, I am surrounded by many lakes. Most of the cabin owners are from Illinois. Everyday I am surrounded by beautiful scenery. If that is not inspiring, then nothing is.

That wasn't the last time that I won something. All my life, good things kept happening. Little did I know that luck did not play a part in my existence. It was the Grace of God.

My dad was always in our lives growing up. I wouldn't see him too often because he had another family. My dad was a hard worker and a good man. One winter my dad was laid off from the railroad. A gas station in town had a contest. If you could carry five hundred silver dollars with one hand for one mile, you would win the $500. These coins weighed thirty-two pounds. My dad won this contest. It was much needed for him and his family. At that time, he had a family with five other kids to support.

One time my brother and I were playing in an old truck that my dad left there. We didn't know it but there was a hornet nest under the dash. When I saw the hornets flying around, we tried to get out. My brother made it out 0k, but I couldn't get my door opened. I got stung over fifty times. My mom came to my rescue and took me down to the lake. She packed mud all over my face. This helped to take the swelling down and draw out the stingers and poison.

We had a lot of bushes close to our lodge and there were plenty of mosquitos around all the time. My mom would hire a man with a tractor to spray DDT. My brother would follow the tractor when it sprayed. He was in the c10Ud of DDT. I was too small, and I couldn't keep up. My mom and brother both died of Parkinson's Disease. The kitchen window was always open, so that is how that cloud of DDT got her.

In the fifties there were no health warnings. We probably handled a lot of things that were harmful. I remember breaking a thermometer to get the mercury out to play with it. No one knew the hazards.

My mom would warn us about bears because from time to time we would see them. One afternoon my brother and I were walking down a dirt road and suddenly two cubs started for us. I said, run Marvin. We ran for a good three or four minutes, then we reached the lodge. One cub was about 30-40 feet behind me. I did stay in for the rest of the day. I didn't want to leave the house for a while. I spent most of my time on the lake. My two favorite things were to fish and water ski. A lot of musky fisherman would take me with them. I saw a lot of muskies in my life. Then they could shoot them in the spine with a pistol. That would paralyze them.

If you never hooked a musky you have missed an experience and a great thrill. That is a sport that is easy to master. I used to do it day after day. I had a few muskies that would pull my boat. I never caught them. I was too small and most of the time they would break my line. My mom always cleaned my fish. She enjoyed doing it. Everyone loved fish and we had it for a meal a few times a week during the summer months. I would bring home 10-15 pan fish every time I went fishing. Living on a chain of five lakes, I knew where to go.

Everyday was fun, we had a field where we played softball. We also played shuffle board, horseshoes, archery and sail boating. We had our own putting green for golf. They were the best years of my life.

Chapter Three

Chased with a butcher knife

My mom sold the resort when I started seventh grade. I lived on the south side of town.

Now instead of having acres and acres to roam around, I had a small lot. I did have neighbor kids to chum around with. It just wasn't the same. Once you live in the country you don't want to live anywhere else. I missed the lake the fishing every day.

It was a shock for me. I met a lot of mean kids around our neighborhood. I had a couple of good friends that I would hang out with. Even living in town, I did what I wanted.

I had to walk a mile each way to school. Rain or snow, we didn't complain, we just did it. That is when people were tough. You didn't dare sass your folks then. If you did you would get whipped. Back then I guess they thought we would learn our lesson, but we never did. You get over pain pretty fast. When we left the resort, that was the last time that I got beat with the switch.

I didn't care for my science teacher. She took some getting used to. Her name was Clair. One day in class I did something that Clair didn't like, so she tried to shame me in front of the class. So I called her Clair in front of the class. As soon as I said that she jumped out of her chair and grabbed a butcher knife that was on the table and proceeded to run towards me. I wasn't going stand there, so I took off running out the door. She chased me down two hallways and another teacher joined in and they finally cornered me. Yes, I was scared, because I didn't know what she was going to do to me. She said, I would like to hurt you but not with this knife. After that I was marched back to the class as if nothing happened.

That is how it was in the sixties. She probably thought that scaring me with that knife was enough punishment.

Some of the teachers thought they were tough. One time I got thrown up against the wall. They got away with a lot of stuff. Now days teachers with these kinds of attitudes and actions would be sued.

Girls had to wear dresses only. Guys always had to have their shirt tucked in. The teachers were strict. I never told my mom when I got in trouble at school. That way she couldn't yell at me. Now if a teacher chased you with a butcher knife, their life would be ruined.

Occasionally someone would pick on me. One guy noticed it and approached me. He said for twenty bucks, I'll be your body guard. I said, 0k. Doug earned his money. If someone would smart off to me, he would jump them. I only had to pay him once.

Junior high wasn't too exciting. There wasn't too much to look forward to. My favorite class was Art. I would get A's and B's. That class was always exciting.

I lived a block from a park. Behind the park was a river. Sometimes I would skip school and I would lay on the river bank until it was time to go home. I did that four or five times. I never did get caught.

Always prayed growing up and I knew God was real at an early age. Without the Lord, I would have never made it. Especially with all the stupid things that I did. God grabbed a hold of me and shook me until I woke up.

The Lord always makes me feel alive. And every day is an adventure. God was very patient with me. I guess he know that there was hope for me after all.

Chapter Four

Bit be a skunk

I always wondered what it would be like to live with my Dad. I lived with my Dad in Minnesota the second half of my junior year and the first half of my senior year.

My carefree life was over now. My Dad had a farm. He had twenty beef cattle and seventeen horses. I had to feed them before and after school. My dad worked on the railroad. I had a stepmother that hated me. I had other stepsisters and one stepbrother. I always loved my stepbrother Bill. He treated me better than anyone. I was so proud of him because he could be a tough guy when he wanted. After he left home, I had to do all the chores. I didn't mind, at least I was away from my stepmother.

You wouldn't believe the emotional abuse I had to deal with. Back then we didn't discuss with anybody about our mental anguish. Now every time you turn around there is someone crying about something.

Occasionally I had to plow or disc a field. I enjoyed that work. We had forty acres of woods. I would often take the rifle with me to go hunting. I was in the woods no longer than five minutes, when I saw something move. I noticed a little skunk. I didn't want to kill him, so I went back home to get a gunny sack from the garage. My plan was to catch him. I got back to the spot where I first saw him, and he was still there. I got down on my hands and knees with the sack opened. He was looking right at me so I knew I wouldn't get sprayed.

I was inching my way closer and closer to him. Not thinking about the consequences. I put the sack in front of him and when I went to scoop him up, he bit my finger. Then I pulled the sack over him and brought him home.

My dad brought the skunk to the University Hospital and they did an autopsy. In the mean while I had to have rabbi shots. Seven in total. One day on one side of my stomach and the next day the other side. If the skunk would have been rabid, I would have had to have seven more shots. Those shots were really painful.

I learned my lesson. I left the animals alone. I was never much of a hunter because I didn't like killing any kind of animals. I didn't feel right about shooting something.

In the summer I had to bale hay. We got payed one dollar an hour and we had to buy school clothes with that money. Life was sure different living with my dad. My mom bought everything for me. I was going backwards.

I knew soon something was going to happen. I was fed up with the farm life and doing all the work. One day I was sitting in my room and I said, help me Lord. I was tired of being treated badly by my stepmother. I knew that I was leaving that day, but I didn't know when or how.

The Lord answered my prayers in ways I would never expect. It was January and around ten above. I put on two pairs of pants and three shirts. I wasn't going to freeze. I needed a good excuse otherwise my dad would come after me.

Little did I know it but at supper time I got my excuse. We were having pizza. I didn't really care for it at all. When she got to the table, she put a piece on my plate and said you are going to eat this. I said, No I am not. After the third time of saying no she picked up the pizza and smeared it all over my face.

My bedroom was right next to the kitchen, so I grabbed my winter coat and ran out the door. I started hitchhiking into town. Town was five miles away. A class mate picked me up and I payed him five bucks to drive me across the state line. At last I was free.

It was nine o'clock at night when I got to St. Croix Falls. It was cold out and I had to think fast. I went to a movie theater and watched the Boston Strangler. After eleven o'clock I had to find a place to get out of the cold. I spotted a laundry mat that was open all night. I slept under one of the folding tables that night and the next morning I made it back to my home with my mom. My dad never did come back for me. I never realized how good I had it until I was away from home.

Life always throws you a few curves and nothing seems to go to your liking. God has always been with me and has never let me down. Sometimes you have to go through hell before you get to heaven.

I had to give my life completely to him before the blessings would occur. God has always been my true friend and the only one I could confide in. It took a long time for me to get where I wanted to be. That is on the right side of God.

I was so glad to see my mom. I missed her meals a lot. Now I was at peace again. No one telling me what to do or getting yelled at. I was a normal person again. I could go where I wanted to go and do what I wanted to do without someone telling me no. A weight was lifted off my shoulders.

Strange occurrences keep occurring time and again. Only the Lord knows what he has in store for me. I'll just have to sit back and relax.

Chapter Five

Five days in Jail for vagrancy

I lived with my brother when I was eighteen. My mom was sick with Parkinson's. My brother treated me bad a lot of times. One day we got into an argument and he threw me out of the house. Literally. It was towards the evening and I had no place to go so I slept in a telephone booth. About three in the morning the cops picked me up and threw me in jail for five days for vagrancy.

When I got out, I had nowhere to go so I hitchhiked to San Francisco. I learned to go to the truck stops because a trucker would take you where you were going most of the way. I got a ride with one trucker who took me from Wisconsin to Portland. I helped him unload his truck in Oregon, he bought me meals and gave me money for helping.

In my travels, I learned how to survive with just the clothes on my back. I learned all the tricks of the trade. Sometimes I spent many hours on the road, just waiting for a ride. I spent all that time talking to God and asking for his help. He never let me down. Even though I didn't live the way he wanted me to, he never gave up on me. God is a loving God and he loves us no matter what.

I learned to go to church because they always help you. When I would get to a town, I would call a Catholic Church. The Catholic's would do more for you than any other denomination. If I was hungry, they would call a restaurant and they would give you a voucher to eat on. For a place to stay they would put you up in a hotel or motel.

If it was too late at night I would go to a jail and they would let you stay overnight. You would have to get fingerprinted first.

There was never a dull moment on the road. A car would stop to pick you up and you would hurry to get to the car and when you got there, they would take off. That would happen more than once.

All the time that I hitchhiked I was never afraid. I feared no one except our Lord. God is the one that we don't want to disappoint. If we are going to get to Heaven, then I've got to live for him completely.

God was patient with me. He knew that I loved him and that is why he blessed me so much. God is worthy of our praise. We must remind him every day how much we love him. When you show him so much love, God will open up to you like nothing you've ever seen.

I met another guy on the road, so I hung around with him for a few weeks. I traveled to Los Angeles with him. If you have never been to Los Angeles, you are not missing anything. Where the bus station is, all the walls and some buildings are so dirty. The town smells. Next to the bus station is a sidewalk filled with drunks and bums lined up for a block long.

We walked by them and they would ask for money. They are all sitting down or laying down. My buddy that I was with got smart with one guy and his buddy reached into his pocket and pulled out a gun. I saw the handle. I had to think fast. I reached into my pocket like I had a gun and the guys partner told him to put the pistol away. I told my buddy, let's get out of here. L.A. was not the place to be. We both decided that we wanted to go to Hollywood.

We both had a few bucks on us so for eight dollars we took a bus. We were eating at a Jack in the Box on Hollywood and Vine and that is not the place you want to be. The place was full of Gays and Lesbians. Outside was a magazine rack a block long. The movie stars and gays would pick up young men or girls.

We went to the Chinese Grumman Theater, they had a free showing of foreign movies and other films. We stayed there for an hour and we left. I only say one movie star while I was there. Betty Grable. I wanted to see more of them, but it didn't happen. We were told to go to the spaghetti factory for a free meal. Certain times the meals were free to the public. We also hit a church for a free meal. My buddy wanted to go to Oregon, and I didn't want to go with him. We then parted ways. I didn't mind because he brought a lot of attention to himself with that hunting knife strapped to his waist.

Sometimes when we hitchhiked, he would have a hard time because he carried a hunting knife strapped to him. He carried this knife for protection, and I had the Lord. The Lord was my protection.

Chapter Six

Held captive by a religious cult

I was on my own again. I liked it better when I was calling the shots. It was starting to get dark and there were a lot of pretty girls downtown talking the work of God. They were Jesus freaks. They worked for Tony and Susan Alamo Ministries. They invited me to a free meal at their compound some fifty miles north of Hollywood in the hills.

They had cars with eight doors. I guess they planned on recruiting a lot of people. They put the pretty girls on the street. That was a trick to get you there. I bit, all I wanted was a free meal so what could it hurt. I didn't know it but if you stayed for supper you couldn't go back to town.

I listened to a seventy-six-piece brass band for an hour. When it was time to eat, they had vegetarian food. I didn't eat a thing. After supper they appointed someone to stay with me. This guy watched me like a hawk. I said to myself, Lord what did I get myself into. They guy says you are with us now.

He took me to a room and the walls were padded. There were benches all around the room. The room was for brain washing. I had to sit on the bench for an hour or so saying praise you Jesus, love you Jesus. For an hour I had to repeat that while I rocked back and forth on the bench. When they came to get me, they sat me at a table and read scriptures to me.

The second night of the same thing, I really started to think on how to get out of there. I had to play their game. I acted like I really enjoyed being there. After this guy was reading scriptures, I told him how much I enjoyed it. I was trying to gain his trust. I guess I got it.

I told him I had to go to the bathroom. The latrine was outside. There was a cliff ten feet high and sixty feet wide. The latrine was carved out of the cliff. I said, God I really got into a mess this time.

I looked up and I saw some roots hanging down. I pulled myself up that cliff to freedom.

I walked through the hills for a good hour before I got down to the road to hitchhike. The Lord was with me and he never gives me more than I can handle. A lady finally picked me up. I told her my story. She said, I was lucky. Some parents tried to get their kids out of there for years but couldn't.

They would hide them at different places. They grew their own food. It was a big operation. Since they kept you there it was free labor for them. It is sad when you must con someone and hide behind the Lord in doing so. Everyone will answer to God someday.

I have thanked my savior many times for that one. It was the toughest situation that I have ever been in. I bet after my escape they cut all of those roots out of the hill. I would love to have seen the expression on the guys face that was watching me when I escaped. I bet he got into a lot of trouble. Anyway, the Lord took care of me just like he continues to do so.

God does get a lot of my time every day. After all he is my best friend. How many people have God as their best friend? No one that I have ever heard of.

The trouble with people today is they don't care enough about him otherwise they would talk about his glory and how they enrich their lives. God wants our full attention. He deserves it!

It was great to get back home. I never talked to anyone about my experiences. I sure didn't want my mom to worry about me. I put that experience out of my mind for years.

I did learn that you can't trust everyone you meet. When a person is young, they are always putting too much trust in someone. I have been conned so many times in my life. It makes you wonder, if you can trust anyone. That is why I put my trust in God. God won't let me down. Sticking with God makes sense to me. Every day is an adventure and God continues to amaze me.

If I didn't put my trust in God, I may have never gotten out of there. God did keep me out of harm's way more than once. I am grateful and I realize I can't just jump into something without thinking it out. If I got in a mess again, I might not be so lucky. You don't realize how many bad people are out there until you get out on your own.

Chapter Seven
Dated girl who killed four people

I would ride around town with a few buddies looking for girls. That was never a problem because there were a lot of younger girls that wanted to party.

Almost everyone smoked weed then and the women wouldn't go out with you if you didn't have a joint. A lot of them anyway.

One afternoon I went uptown, and I saw this cute red head sitting on the corner, so I went and said hi to her. That was the start of a new romance. I've always been partial to read heads, there is just something about them that turns me on.

Kathy would baby sit for this family that had three kids. On the weekends I would go over there and make time with her when the kids took a nap. I went out with her three or four times then I didn't see her for three years.

When I married my second wife, Kathy lived in the house behind mine. I went outside one day and into my back yard, there she was fifty feet away in her bikini.

I never told my wife that I had gone out with her before. Somethings are better left unsaid.

I learned that while she was babysitting for that same family, she would smoke cigarettes while she was there. She didn't know it, but a cigarette fell into the couch. She went home without realizing it. Early that next morning the house burned to the ground. The father made it out, but the mother and the three kids didn't. Imagine how Kathy felt. I never saw Kathy again. She had a hard pill to swallow and I hope she doesn't dwell on the guilt. Things happen beyond our control sometimes.

Tragedy can strike anyone. If something like that don't scar you for life, nothing will. We never know if tomorrow will be our last day on earth or not. Anything is possible and anything can happen.

That is why it is so important to get right with God. Not only will you feel one hundred percent better, but you will lead a much fuller life.

I know with God I don't have to worry about a thing. Being the jealous God that he is, I must give him as much time as I can to please him. After all God is my best friend.

I know that God would never turn his back on me. He never left me when I did bad things. I guess he figured sooner or later I would come around. All my life I knew right from wrong. I just tried to take shortcuts to get ahead and all it got me was thrown in the Big House.

I was too stubborn. All my life it gave me great pleasure to do nice things for people. There are always a few bad apples that would try to take advantage of your generosity. I can see right through people. I've always been a good judge of character. I distance myself from that kind of element now.

I've been clean for over forty years now and God assures me that I can't go backwards again. Those bad thoughts of getting in trouble and all the other stupid things that I did, don't even enter my mind. I don't have time for that nonsense. God filled that empty void that I had. I always felt like there was something missing. My life wasn't clicking like I wanted it to.

When I gave my life to God, that is when things started to click. My whole outlook on life took a turn for the better. I am a more patient person now. I always wanted things to happen right away. That logic is what got me into trouble in the first place... Things will happen, and I just have to wait for them to take their course.

Chapter Eight

How I met my first wife

The summer of sixty-nine I worked for the Institute of Forest Genetics. I would work with scientists in the radiation fields or in the lab making aluminum vials or whatever. It was something different every day it was always interesting.

I had to walk five miles to work every day. Sometimes I would get a ride. I always started to work an hour early. I loved that job. I screwed up, I had a dream job and I quit to hitchhike to Florida. I wanted to see the country.

The first night I made it to Milwaukee. I was walking through town and I approached this bar and a drunk came out and knocked me on my butt. I got up and he went the other way. I got to the edge of town and I got a motel room for the night. You never know what to expect when you are on the road.

The next day I hooked up with someone that was headed to Florida also. He used to go to St. Leo's College in Dade City. That is where we were headed. He said we could stay at the dorms for a week or so because school was out on vacation.

The next night we made it to Somerset, Kentucky. We rented a hotel room for the night, it cost me two dollars. We bought our carton of cigarettes in Kentucky because it only cost two dollars and fifty cents. Very cheap.

We made it to Dade City, I hung around there for three days. I went there in the wrong time of the year. The temperature was in the nineties. I left by myself and headed back to Wisconsin.

A few days later I was in Muskogee, IL. I was walking through a bad part of town and I saw something I didn't want to see. It was three o'clock in the morning, I stayed in the shadows for a while. I got out of there as quick as I could.

You don't know nothing until you get out and travel around the country. You have to learn how to survive in any situation you get into.

One night I got stuck in the middle of nowhere, it was windy and chilly. I had to go into the woods and pick up broken limbs or whatever to make a shelter for the night. It worked and I didn't freeze.

After being home for a few months a friend talked me into going to vocational school in a town two hours away.

When I got there, I didn't know where to go. I had no money, so I went to the nearest police station. An officer took me to a boarding house. I had to start school the next day.

A blind lady owned and operated the boarding house. She did the cooking, the laundry and sewed our clothes. She did it all.

There were ten of us that stayed there. I fit in pretty good. I made some good friends there. We lived by a high school so the girls would walk by every day. We got to know a lot of them. There were six of us that hung around together. One day we got the idea to all dress alike. We all wore the same clothes when out to bars. One day we would wear blue bell bottom jeans with a gray t-shirt or white bell bottoms with a blue t-shirt.

Everyone was curious when we walked in the door. We had people buying us beers and girls wanting to dance. I lived in a college town and the bars were great. We had fun entertaining ourselves. Some nights we pulled pranks. We would take a swing set from one neighbors' yard and put it across the street in someone else's yard. We did that with outdoor furniture, bird baths or whatever. It was harmless fun.

One day, my friend Lee wanted me to go on a canoe trip with him and two others. It was a three-day trip for one hundred and twenty miles. I like an adventure from time to time, so I went. We had two canoes and we traveled forty miles a day. At night we would sit around the campfire and socialize with other campers. We only got stuck in the rapids once. It was scary enough. We met a lot of nice people along the river. A group of doctors flagged us down and cooked us steaks. We had a good time.

On the last day we had twenty miles to go so the guys in the other canoe snuck up to a dock early in the morning and stole a small outboard motor. They towed us the rest of the way.

I was bored one day so I got the phone book and I started to call people. When they answered, I would say is your daughter home. After the fourth try, one lady said who Karen, and I said yes. She wasn't home so I called back later. That is how I met my first wife. What was most surprising was that she only lived a block away. Six months later we got married.

Karen's Dad was a supervisor for a factory. So, he made sure I had a good job. We made golf club heads. My job was to cut the snub off the wood. The cutting needed to be precise. I did that job half of the night and the other half of my shift I ran the presses.

I got along good with my father-in-law. He took me fishing and it was the best day ever. It was ninety that day and I was using a fluorescent colored daredevil. In a few hours I caught eleven northern. They were all keepers.

Karen and I had a beautiful son together. Our marriage lasted for a few years. She left me for an older guy who owned a home. Once someone cheats on you the trust is gone. My son was the only important part of my life.

I started to hang around the wrong crowd. At that low point in my life, I didn't give the Lord that much time. I was too busy being angry. I was in a rut that I couldn't seem to find my way out of.

I created my own hell when I didn't have time for God. Nothing went right and I didn't care. I was left with that attitude. It took a long time to get over it.

Chapter Nine

Brought minor across State line

The town that I lived in had a library on the corner of the main street. It had a wall a block long. On weekends the girls would sit on the wall waiting to be picked up. I met five or six women that way.

One gal was from a town sixteen miles away. She drove a sixty-four Mustang. I went out with her for a week. I talked her into going to Arizona with me. We brought my buddy along. We probably had sixty bucks between us.

My buddy robbed a few places the night before we left. We would always sell merchandise at pawn shops. I didn't get into the burglary thing right away. I was more of the look out person. We robbed places all the way to Arizona.

Occasionally an easy target would present itself. We stopped at a rock and gift shop. The lady that owned the shop was a little crazy. She would talk to space aliens. I told my girl and my buddy to go out in the back with her and look at the rocks on the tables. It was one hundred feet from the building.

I went out the front door and got my duffel bag. I emptied the till and went to the display cases and loaded my bag up with jewelry, rings, and necklaces. A lot of turquoise and silver jewelry. Also, over one hundred jackknives. We would throw them at telephone polls along the road as we drove. I also went into her living quarters and took an old antique clock off her wall. I found big chunks of turquoise too.

We knew that if she called the cops they wouldn't come because she had called them before about aliens. My girlfriend drove most of the way. She was the only one who had a driver's license.

I would spend some time alone with my girl and my buddy would have to take a hike for a while. We were out in the desert one day and it was quite hot. My buddy took a little walk so we could be alone. When he returned to the car, he was sick from the heat. It got hot in Arizona. The heat was dry, but you felt it. We did a lot of sightseeing along the way.

We left Arizona and headed for Nevada. We got into Boulder City that night. We were getting low on cash. We stayed at a motel every night. We drove around for a bit looking for a place to rob. My girl was now the lookout so that made things easier for us.

We found an antique shop. We parked a block away. That place had three doors. We got the first two opened and it was taking a while for the third door, so I said let's go and take a break. We got back to the car and opened a can of cold beans. After we ate, we drove up town. We didn't know it but in Nevada they had an eleven o'clock curfew. If you were under eighteen you couldn't be on the streets. My girlfriend was driving when we were pulled over. They had a warrant for by buddy, so they flew him back to Wisconsin.

My girlfriend's aunt from Phoenix picked her up. That left me alone. I went to court and they gave me two weeks in jail for bringing a minor across state line. That seemed like the longest two weeks of my life. When I got out, I headed for Phoenix. When I got to Phoenix that night, I headed for the bus station. People would hang out there that had nowhere to go. It saved me from the cold more than once.

Being on the road you never know where your next meal is coming from. Some days I would panhandle for money. You learn what or what not to say. One day I was asking for change and an old lady asked me what I need the money for. I said something to eat. She took me to a restaurant and bought me a meal. After I was done another lady asked me the same thing. I told her something to eat, she took me to a café, and I ate the same thing and a man asked me the same question. He took me to eat. I was stuffed. The next time I asked for money, I told them I needed the money to pay my rent.

Chapter Ten

Matched the description of a cop killer

I hung around with a few other guys that were without a place to stay. Occasionally we would sleep in the park. There was a rescue mission in town that I would stay at occasionally. Everyone had to sleep on the floor. It was uncomfortable but at least I got out of the cold. No blankets and no pillows, just the clothes you were wearing. You tried to sleep with one eye opened. Thirty or so people would crash there. All walks of life. You had to be careful. You trust no one.

These people are all survivors and they will do what they must to survive. You must watch your back all the time. You learn a lot living on the streets. It's no life for anyone. Some of the people would hurt you for your shoes.

I seem to get into circumstances the I shouldn't. At that time in my life I didn't give God much time. How could things get better if God wasn't in my life every day.

When you are young you don't use your brain like you should and you rush into things without thinking about the consequences.

Here I was laying on the floor just getting ready to go to sleep when two cops came in. They had a flashlight and were shining it in everyone's faces. When they got to me, they asked me to step outside. When they got outside, they looked at me again and then looked at each other. I said what is going on? One cop told me I matched the description of a guy that killed two cops. I asked them when did this happen? They told me and I said I can prove where I was when that happened.

They took me to the bus station where I kept me duffel bag in a locker. I showed them that I was locked up when that happened. They took me to a café and bought me a cup of coffee. When I got back to the mission it was locked. I ended up sleeping under a tree that night.

I have been in a lot of tight spots in my life and if not for the

Lord looking over me, I would have never made it.

I wanted to see the country when I was young. I didn't know that a lot of crazy things would happen. I had to learn how to survive and deal with all walks of life.

What if I hadn't had an alibi? I probably would still be in jail. You don't have to look for trouble because a lot of times it finds you. Phoenix was getting old and I thought that it was time to head back to Wisconsin.

Just when I wanted to head out, I met this girl. Her boyfriend was in jail for a while, so I guess she was lonely. She was beautiful. She liked to get stoned and she wasn't bashful. I hung out with her for a few weeks then her boyfriend got out of jail. It was now time for me to move on.

Now I could head back to Wisconsin. I thought so anyway. Life seemed to always throw me a curve ball. I always ended up doing things that I didn't plan.

When you are young you want to believe in people. It seems every where you go, you run into someone that tries to scam you or someone else. I put my trust into people that I shouldn't have. Luckily, I got out of those situations.

Chapter Eleven

Courier for the mob

I was in a Hotel bar and there was a bunch of business men at a table all having drinks. I walked by their table and one guy asked me where I was from. I told him Rhinelander, Wisconsin. He said, Rhinelander, I used to live on Thayer St. When they say it is a small world, sometimes it seems to be true. At least in this respect.

They invited me to their table for drinks and I guess they liked me cause the guy offered me a job, I couldn't refuse. I could have but I never turn down good money. Some of the guys were in the mob. They wanted me to be a courier. They said I would travel to different towns and deliver money to different places. I said, OK. I was young and it was an opportunity to make a few grand a week. In the seventies, that was a lot of money. The next day I got on a bus with another guy and we headed to Blythe, California. He got us a motel room when we got there.

The next day I was supposed to be with someone to show me the ropes. The guy that I was with turned out to be a drunk. What a jerk. He said now you are going to listen to me, and you are going to give me some of the money that you make. He went on and on and started to call me names as he became drunker.

I wasn't going to put up with a drunk. I told him I was going to go out and get a soda. Because he didn't want me to leave, I went and got the manager. He went with me to get my clothes and I started back to Phoenix.

I thanked the Lord for getting me out of that mess. Things would have gone south if I would have stuck around. I wasn't going to take crap from anyone, no matter who it was. I made wrong choices just because I thought I could make easy money. If it sounds to good to be true, it isn't. I ran across so many scam artists in my life.

You just can't trust anyone. Even in the sixties the world was just as crazy. Now there are a lot of mentally disturbed people out there.

I was headed back to Phoenix and then on to Wisconsin. I got side tracked, one more time. Two girls and a guy picked me up and the guy was a hitchhiker too. He was headed to Dateland, Arizona and had a job there. These girls were going to take him all the way. They guy asked if I wanted a job, so I said yes. Ten minutes later these girls fired up a joint and passed it around. When we got there, our beds were our sleeping bags. They had a mess hall for the meals.

I worked on the cotton fields, I put the irrigation systems together and made sure the water was irrigating. I loved the job. It would reach one hundred and twenty degrees on the desert. You couldn't have your shirt off for more than twenty minutes or your skin would be like an alligator.

This place that I worked for was know for hiring illegal aliens. The border patrol would come once a week. Those that they found would get deported and three days later they would be back.

They made good money here and they would send it back to Mexico. I saw a lot of them that were married have girl friends here and the girls would know they were married.

There was a bar twenty miles away out in the middle of nowhere. There wasn't another bar around for a hundred miles. Most of the time you stayed inside after work. Working in the hot sun all day took a lot out of your body. You didn't feel like doing much at the end of the day.

Whenever you had to lift one of the irrigation pipes you needed to be careful because a lot of the times a rattle snake would be curled up under it. I only saw a few snakes but, you always had to be aware of your surroundings.

Sunday was the only day that we didn't work. One Sunday we were all sitting around outside, and this truck shows up pulling a small camping trailer. It was a guy and his family that moved from Oregon. He was hired to drive tractor for the season.

I couldn't believe the words that came out of his mouth. He had a seventeen-year-old daughter and he said, if anyone wants to have sex with my daughter, that's 0k with me. I knew that that this guy had a few screws loose to say that. It had been a while since I saw a girl. You can imagine what goes through a guy's mind.

Saturday, I had a guy drive me to the bar. I bought a case of beer and when I got back, I knocked on that guys door. I gave him the case of beer. I didn't know what else to do because I had never been in a situation like that. He told me that I didn't need to buy any beer. I told him I wanted to. We sat around for a while and I got to know his daughter.

I wasn't shy. I didn't have to be told twice. We went outside to her camping trailer where we had some privacy. There was a swimming pool and the girl would jump in to cool off.

It made my job more interesting. Every night I was there I would spend with her. I had her Dad's blessing. He like me. After the season was over, I was heading back to Wisconsin. That girl and her family were going back to Oregon and they wanted me to go with them. I told him I had to go back home.

I didn't need another adventure. I wanted to go home. I had a few buddies that I hung around with, one of them was A1, his mother was the head of the hospital. She was always giving him money, so there was always a good party. I couldn't find any work so I thought I would get out of the cold for the winter.

Chapter Twelve
Beat up be Ex Hells Angel

After taking a bus part way I ended up in Albuquerque, New Mexico. I met this woman on the bus that had the same birthday as mine. She was six years older than me. She had just got divorced from her lawyer husband. I spent all day at her place. She was a nice woman. I didn't want to get into a relationship, so I left.

I mad it to Berkley, California and I ended up in Richmond. They had a mission there where I stayed for a month. You had to work for a few hours a day. Once a week I would ride to Berkley or Oakland to pick up food for the mission. You would always see Hells Angels all day long.

A lot of times I would sit around the lounge area. I would watch this guy picking up cigarette butts off the floor. I felt sorry for him, so I walked over to him and handed him a cigarette. He said thanks. I would give him a smoke every time that I saw him. A person does have to have a heart. It did pay off being nice to him.

I hung around with a guy named Fred. He was a big guy. One day we were in the office and I was typing a letter back home. In the room came an ex hells angel. He got kicked out of the club because when he got drunk, he would go crazy and want to fight everyone. I said, I am writing a letter back home. He said, why? I told him because I wanted to. Then he hauled off and hit me while I was sitting in my chair. Then he told me to hit him, I said No. The he hit me in the head again. I knew that I need to do something. I said, God help me. I wasn't looking for trouble and I found it. The third time that he hit me in the head, I fell off the chair and played possum. At that time the guy that I gave a cigarette to jumped him. I got up and ran upstairs. Fred was behind me and he locked the door.

In the meanwhile, I opened the window and climbed down two stories until I reached the ground. When I reached the ground, I reached the next block. I stopped and knocked on a door to use their phone.

This black chic answers and asks me what is the password? I said, I don't know any password, I just want to use the phone. She shut the door on me. I was walking a bit and I saw that guy that assaulted me in the back of a police car.

When I got back to the mission, Fred told me he mixed ammonia and water together and when that guy pounded on his door, Fred opened it and threw the ammonia in his face and called the cops. Fred was a coward while the guy was punching me. He made up for it. I didn't hang around with him much longer. He didn't have much ambition and I didn't want to hang around some one that only thinks of them self. When you hang around with some one for a while you learn what they are about fast. I always did much better by myself.

I headed for the bus depot. I would meet people that just got off the bus. I would meet more girls that way. A hell angel walked up to me and asked me where I was from. I told him. He told me that I looked like a guy that beat up one of the hells angels' mother. I talked to him for a while. Then he left. Things always happen to me. I don't know why, but they just do.

California wasn't too good to me... I got back home and met a girl downtown. I went out with her for a few months. She then moved to Minneapolis with her cousin. They planned to live together when they got out of school A month later, I moved to Minneapolis and I moved in with them. Now, I was living with two girls. We all had jobs during the day. I worked at a pickle factory twenty blocks away. None of us had a car so we walked every where we had to go. I was there six months and my girl, and I decided to move back to Wisconsin. So, we did, and we moved to my home town.

Chapter Thirteen
Robbed a bank

I did get my girlfriend pregnant. We ended up going to Minneapolis to get married. They didn't have a waiting period in that state like some states you have to wait five to ten days after filing. We went to the court house and paid the Judge to marry us. He asked where our witnesses were. We didn't have any. I ended up going out into the hallway and asked two women to be our witnesses. They agreed so ten minutes later we were married.

Her family was religious. She was the rebellious one of her family. I got along good with her parents. They were good people and always a pleasure to be around. They lived in the country on a farm. He had a garden and grew the best potatoes.

We would most likely end up there after church on Sunday. There was nothing like a home cooked meal. She had a lot of sisters and brothers. Three or four of them went to Bible College. One of them was a missionary. There were always different church functions to go to. A lot of times my wife and I wouldn't see eye to eye. We were both stubborn. We were both Tauruses.

A lot of our problems were about money. I didn't always work steady all the time. When you are young you don't think about serious things that much. When you are young you don't have a care in the world.

I tried to make sure that my wife and son had what they needed. Sometimes you try to hard. I always wanted to give them a better life. One day I would get the opportunity to, with our realizing it.

It was January and it was cold out. It was a Saturday late afternoon, my wife asked me to go over to one of her brothers to paint their bedroom. I didn't want to, but I got talked into it. Her younger brother showed up to help also. Her older brother that we painted for was also the black sheep of the family. We were drinking beer while we painted. That night it was snowing hard. We were getting a little drunk. I don't remember much about the painting.

I mentioned to my brother-in-law that I had a key to the bank. He said good, lets rob it and I said, 0k. That is how that got started.

Three nights before that I was calling psychics and telling them I had money problems. One psychic told me in three days all my problems would be solved. They were solved alright, the third day I robbed the bank.

I used to work for a cleaning service that cleaned the bank. There were no alarms on the building only in the safe. The front or back doors did not have alarms. Before I quit, I had an extra key made in case I lost mine. I just kept the extra key at the time I never thought about robbing it. It was a very stupid thing to do.

The night after we left my older brother-in-law house, my younger brother-in-law and wife headed back to my house. We had to have a plan before we went in. They had eight till drawers, so I brought a screwdriver to pry them open. One night my boss told ne when she got to work, she found fifty thousand that they left out. She called the manager and he came down and locked it up in one of the till drawers.

I knew that there was change in the drawers, but I thought they had cash too. I don't know how many thousands in coins we got. The bank never tells the truth when they get robbed. My wife gave me an old canvas purse to put a lot of the coins in. She knew what her brother and me were doing. But when we got caught, everything was my fault. Her father wanted me to tell the cops that the whole idea was mine. I was the bad guy. I kept my wife from getting into trouble.

I never mentioned her helping me with different things. We were stupid when we got caught. We were sixty miles away the next day. He was taking me to the airport when we stopped in town. We never thought nothing of it because we were a way away. We went to a few stores and cashed in a few rolls of quarters. After a few minutes we headed back to our car. After we got in the car, an FBI agent put a gun to my head and told me to get out of the vehicle.

He threw me to the ground and put me in cuffs. I thought I would be locked up for a while. My brother-in-law got six months' probation and I got eighteen months in prison. After a month, I got sent to a prison camp, seventy miles away. My wife would take my son with her and visit me every weekend. I always mad sure she had a ride. I had a good friend that helped us out.

The state got me a job the third day after I was released. They didn't want me to get into trouble again. In the seventies the state cared about you. Now most everyone is hateful.

After being home for a year or so, I guess I was just tired of being told what to do. My wife didn't want me to smoke in the house. I had to go to church three times a week. Her whole family belonged to the Assembly of God. Everything revolved around her and her family. I always came second.

One day I just got fed up with her yelling. The next day was Sunday and when it was time to go to church, I told her I was sick. I got on a bus and headed for Arkansas. Fifty miles before Little Rock a young girl gets on the bus and sits right next to me. She asked me for a cigarette. She was headed to Little Rock also. She was friendly with me and it was obvious what was going to happen once we got to town.

Things always have a way of happening to me. I don't mind if they are good but in a lot of circumstances it doesn't turn out that way. We went to a restaurant and I bought her a steak dinner and after dinner I got us a hotel room.

The reason I went to Little Rock was to get out of the cold weather. It was just as cold there. This girl was way out there. She was talking about me pimping her off. She was going to make money for me. I never expected that talk out of her. I always said you don't know nothing about life until you get out on your own.

I was a little nervous and I walked a block and picked up a bottle of wine. I wasn't used to just meeting some one and getting to know them better. I got to thinking during the night, I have to get out of this one. I sure didn't want to be a pimp.

Morning came and I said I'll get us breakfast and I'll see you soon. I went right to the bus station and took a bus to Dallas, Texas.

I got to that town and I said no thank you. There was so many people, not for me. My dad lived in Arizona, so I went to see him. He owned an antique business. While I stayed with him, I got a job as a salesman. I sold fuller brush. I lived in a Mormon community so the women would like to buy. I was proud of that job. For one month, I was number three for selling fuller brush in the whole state of Arizona.

There were a lot of friendly women. One black chic fired up a joint as soon as I sat down. I guess she thought all of us white guys got high. After I left her place I had to sit on the side of the road for an hour. You never know what to expect.

I made my deliveries on Saturdays. I went to one house to deliver and this gal opened her robe and had nothing on but a smile. She glanced out the window and saw my wife and sister in the car. She closed her robe and paid me for the products she had ordered. Then I left. Not another word was spoken.

I eventually moved back to my home town. That's one thing you can always go home.

Chapter Fourteen

Cop busted me having sex with his daughter

My buddy and I would go to different bars in towns twenty-five miles away. We always looked for girls. In the late sixties and early seventies were the best years. There were no DUI's if you were driving, they would take your beer away and tell you to drive home.

We were drinking at this one bar, and I noticed a girl sitting alone so I went over and introduced myself. I bought her a drink. She came and sat with me. A half hour later she was sitting on my lap. I told my buddy I had a ride home. He was jealous and begged me to go with him. I wasn't stupid. She took me home and I had a new girlfriend. I don't think I hung around with my buddy after that. I didn't need to look for any more women.

She lived fifty miles away. Neither one of us had a car. I would hitchhike on Friday night to see her and Sunday night she would take me home in her dads' car. This went on for two to three months. I would sleep on their couch. Her mother would fix breakfast before she left for work. She was a postmaster general. Occasionally her folks would take me out for supper. Here dad was a cop and he was retired for a little while.

He now would fiberglass boats and sell them. I helped him one day. It was pretty interesting. I got along good with her dad. Sometimes he would take me out in his boat. She was in the service and had just gotten out. She was paid good from the service, around eight-hundred a month. That was good money back then. She did spoil me. She wasn't too honest though.

She knew that I liked antiques. Before she would take me home, she took me to a few cabins that I broke into. It seemed like everyone I met was into breaking and entering. When her dad was on the force, she would ride along with him to check on cabins and so forth. She knew who was home or not.

One weekend I should have stayed home. I got there on Friday night and the next morning her dad was headed to the marina to work on a boat. After he left, we started to make love on the couch. Two minutes later he walked in and busted me making love to his daughter.

He walked right by us and went to his bedroom. If looks could kill, then I would have been dead. I'm lucky he didn't tear my head off. That would be a bad situation for any man to be in, catching his daughter in the act. I had to stay there seven more hours before she would take me home. I've never been so embarrassed in my life.

When his wife got home, he whispered something to her. I had to eat supper therebefore my girl would take me home. That was the worst feeling in the whole world. At supper no one said a word. After I ate, I went out on the porch until she took me home. I never did go back there. I couldn't face those people.

My girl would come and see me. I went with her for another month. Then I met another woman. This woman was a red head that I met in a bar. She was not the kind of woman that you want to take home to mom.

Her whole life was drinking so I knew this relationship wasn't going to go very far. I was at a low point in my life where not much mattered.

One night at a bar I met a guy and we talked about doing some burglaries. We smoked a joint and the following day we planned to meet up.

Chapter Fifteen

Sixty counts of burglaries

I was a burglar in the seventies and a darn good one. My down fall was having a partner. We would go out from eight thirty to eleven thirty in the morning and I always stuck to that plan. Back then you could fool people pretty easy. We only did our crimes in the country.

One time by myself I knocked on a door and a lady answered. I asked for so and so and she didn't know. I asked her, what about the people down the road, would they know? She said, no they are both working. So, I left and went down the road and pulled into the drive way.

I kicked the back door. In the bedroom I found a manila envelope full of cash. I was in and out in less than three minutes. The sooner you get out the better. When you do a crime with someone else, you let your guard down. You never rely on someone else. It proved to be very costly for me. I told my partner to only take cash. We wouldn't take jewelry either. I didn't want nothing traceable. My partner wouldn't listen. He would take chainsaws and other things.

The day that we got busted he brought a pistol with him He never did that before. He had bib overalls on and the pistol in his back pocket. There is a saying, if you ever draw your gun, you had better be prepared to use it. Well, he wasn't.

We drove twenty-five miles to another town. We were high. I had a bag of weed on me, so we were feeling our oats. We smoked a lot of joints.

The first place we got too was about a mile out of town. The door was unlocked. We went in to the first bedroom. My buddy was supposed to watch out the window. We both had a dresser on each side to go through. He was supposed to be looking out the window.

I was going through the drawers and I found a pair of women's panties. I said to my buddy, look at this. At that moment a guy walked in and said what are you doing? I said looking for someone. He said bull shit. I whispered to my partner to shoot him, shoot him. My buddy shook his head no.

We ran out the door and got ten miles down the road before we got pulled over. Before we got stopped, I grabbed the gun and threw it in the snow bank. I knew better and I got rid of it. My partner was stupid. His lawyer used to be a DA and told him to spill his guts. All they had on us was one count of attempted burglary.

My partner wrote out a statement against me and I got six years. He was given three years and was sent to a different prison. When you are incarcerated you must always watch your back.

I got a job on the yard crew. What I liked about that was that I had a weapon all the time that I was working. I had a long stick with a nail on the end and a bag for picking up trash. Sometimes I had a pair of garden shears for cutting the grass. I only had to use it on one inmate. I was working close to a building and this black guy grabbed me, so I stuck him with the shears. He backed off all right.

Only one time I was a little worried. We on the rec field, there were ten of us. We were surrounded by twenty black inmates. The tallest guy stood right by my side. I wasn't worried, I had my stick with the nail in it. He stood next to me and I looked at him with a smirk on my face. I looked at him and at the same time I was shoring up my stick. A few minutes later the guard broke it up.

Once I got stabbed with a pencil. The lead stayed in my arm for a while. There are a lot of things you must learn fast. Sometimes you had to go with the flow. There aren't that many guards watching you. One time I walked in on a blanket party. I had to join in other wise they would turn on me.

About six to eight inmates would cover a guy they didn't like with the blanket. They would put a bar of soap in their sock or a padlock. They would beat him with that for a few minutes. They never hit him in the face. That was always the rule. You would kill some one if you did that. I only got invited to two parties. I never enjoyed that.

After being locked up for a few years, I got moved to the dorm. It was an open area with eighty beds. One guard on each end of the room. Downstairs were showers, pool tables, ping pong and a boxing ring. If you had a beef with someone, they allow you to box it out. One guy got smart with me, so I challenged him, and he accepted.

I knew I was going to win. I had a lifer train me. He would never get out as he killed two people. In the second round I gave him an upper cut. He was seeing stars and said, I quit. There must have been twenty people around the ring. They were all shouting finish him, finish him. I couldn't be like that. I proved my point.

After another year I went to a prison camp close to my home. It was nice to have more freedom again.

Chapter Sixteen

Escaped from prison

I always kept my mind occupied. I had around ten women I wrote to all the time. I put ads in different papers, even easy rider. Some would visit me, and some would send me money. I was writing a French girl in New York, she had a good job. She was a director for a nursing home. She would send me cash. There are a lot of lonely women out there.

When I first got to the prison camp, I got approached by two guys that wanted to escape. They said you know this area so if you ever want to go, we are in. At the time I wasn't thinking about escaping. It had never entered my mind.

I worked on the DNR crew trimming trees. I had a long pole with a saw on the end. I sawed a branch and the next thing that happened, a hornet stung me on the eye lid. Talk about pain, I went right to my knees. I couldn't see out of that eye for two hours. Two guys had to carry me out of the woods. They took me to a clinic, I wore a patch for a few days. One day it was so hot and miserable. It was my dad's birthday, August 5th.

Things would just happen, I wouldn't plan them. I walked up to the two guys and I said we are leaving tonight. They said, 0k. I told them you are going to listen to me. They said, 0k. They wanted to steal a car, I said are you crazy? I told them we are going down the river, we are going to steal a canoe. That is what we did.

We had to swim across the river to get in a garage to get a canoe. I almost didn't make it. We didn't have anything to eat for three days. The first night we hid out in the woods about five miles away.

We were running through the woods right away to put some distance between us. I was running and then all of a sudden, I ran into a stump. Boy did that hurt. I had a limp for three weeks. My knee was killing me. Hurt or not I had to keep going. Once we got the canoe, we had eighty miles to travel.

One of the guys was writing an older woman so we headed there. We got to my home town. We were on our way to Portage. To make it to Portage we had to get our canoe a mile and a half further down river. Suddenly, a man with a pick-up said do you boys need to get to Portage, we said yes. We put our canoe in his truck and he drove us a mile and a half around town so we could get our canoe back in the river to continue our trip. The guy that helped us turned out to be the brother of the Sheriff.

After a half hour of canoeing we pulled up into the woods. We only canoed at night when it was dark. I was in charge, so I always had to think fast.

It was fall so most of the cabins were empty. We did spend the night in one cabin to get out of a rain storm. Being on the run wasn't fun. I often said to myself, what did I get myself into this time.

God would let me make my own mistakes. He probably said to himself, will he ever learn? God was more than patient with me. He had to be. That is why he is my best friend. God stuck with me no matter what. He must had seen promise in me. He must have wondered when I would grow up.

We got caught in a thunder storm one night, so we got to shore and tipped the canoe over and got under it. We still were soaked, and we stayed that way for twelve hours or so. We went through hell sometimes, but I didn't mind as I was free, and I intended to keep it that ways.

We broke into one cabin and the guys grabbed three bottles of booze. Those guys drank but I didn't. I wasn't going to let my guard down.

We did get caught in the rapids one time and the canoe did tip over close to shore. It was no picnic.

It was a good thing that we all wrote to women. We couldn't have made it with out their help. We finally made it to our destination. We were walking down an industrial part of town and we saw a cop that was headed our way. The other two took off running and made it back to the river. That was our safe zone.

The cop told me to come here so I went up to his window and he told me to get in the car. I said no and I took off running. I couldn't run too fast cause I had that limp. I was running through yards and a guy was watering his lawn, he said go this way. He helped me to get away. I made it back to the river and we stayed by the river until it was dark.

A few hours later we made it to that woman's house. She let us stay there for a week. The woman I was writing to sent me two hundred dollars western union in that lady's name. She picked up the money for me and got me a bus ticket to New York.

The next day she took me to the bus station, and I was on my way. I found out the other two guys did a burglary and got caught. One guy got his leg broken by a cop who really nailed him hard with his flashlight.

We all needed each other to escape but when I got to my destination, that was a different story.

Chapter Seventeen
Made it to New York

Here I am on the subway and sitting across from me is a cop. Needless to say, I was a little paranoid. I finally made it to eighty second street in Brooklyn. Maria was at an office party and left the door open for me. I had to wait three more hours to finally see her.

She left a joint for me to smoke. I got a good buzz, so I got in the tub to relax. It had been a while since I was able to do that. She finally came home, and we had quite a time. After a week of relaxing, I got myself a job. I had a fake ID made and I went by the name of Mike Logan. For the first couple of months, I worked for a landscaper. It was a fun job. We would work mostly in Brooklyn and Stanton Island.

Larry was a good boss. Every week he would take me to a different place. We would go golfing one week and the next week we would go to the Belmont race track. A lot of the times Caravel Ice Cream would be on my boss's mind. It was the best tasting ice cream I ever had. That is the only thing that I miss about New York.

My girlfriends' best friend was a Puerto Rican and her husband ran a street gang. We were at their house drinking rum and coke and after an hour or so he took me and introduced me to his gang. It was three in the morning and I was kind of nervous. I told him I escaped from prison. He said, don't worry no one will bother you.

The leader was a real nice guy and he treated me good. I asked some of the guys why they stood on the street corner all night. One guy told me that they were guarding their turf. They didn't like anyone invading their turf. The gang members that I talked to were really nice and some were family men. Just because you belong to something doesn't make you a bad person.

After three months we got into an argument and she wanted me out. The next day I rented a room. I went back to her place to get my clothes, so I had to wait for her to get home. I was just sitting there, and four FBI agents came out from nowhere and the threw me to the ground.

It was all over, she had turned me in. I was just sick to my stomach. The cops didn't know where to take me. First, they took me to the metropolitan correctional institution. That was a federal prison and I didn't belong there. Next, they took me to Rikers Island. I was there for a little while and I didn't belong there. I was glad to get out of there. It is the worst jail in the United States. That is a fact. They let you wear your own clothes there and people have been killed for their tennis shoes.

I thanked God when I got out of there.

They finally took me to the Brooklyn House of Detention. I looked out the window and I saw the Statue of Liberty. How neat was that. They put me on the tenth floor with the escapees and murderers. For entertainment they had a room for us to watch movies.

Our cells were open during the day so we could visit. A few guys did get me high. No matter where you went there was always pot. The guards would bring a lot of pot in. That was the only way you could relax in there.

After a month they flew me back to Wisconsin. I was glad to be back. I had my freedom and now it was time to finish my sentence. I got an extra two and a half years for the escape. After a year I got sent to a medium security prison. Where I was incarcerated, we had miniature golf. I would play that every day. I only had to work two hours a day and then I could do what I wanted. It was the best place to do time. I would hang around with an inmate named Johnny. He was an armed robber that would hold up drug stores.

Ed a biker that belonged to an out-law gang would get us high. If you have never been high before, you will if you go to prison. No one knows what to expect because things are beyond your control.

After spending a year there, I was finally paroled. And I have not been in trouble since. All together I wasted six years of my life. I did learn from my experiences. Crime doesn't enter my thoughts anymore. I was out of prison for good now. God is the only one that keeps me on the right path.

Chapter Eighteen
Moved to Arizona

Once I got home, I had my parole officer transfer me to Arizona. I went to live with my dad. I got a job driving a frontend loader for a potting soil plant. My dad bought me a car so I could get around. I lived in a small town and it connected to another town.

They had a female cop that drove back and forth between those towns. I would follow her all over. She knew I had a crush on her. One time I followed her, she turned on the sirens and pulled me over. When I stopped, she drove right on by? Roberta was her name.

I didn't play cat and mouse with her too much longer. I didn't want to start a relationship with her because I didn't want her to know that I was in prison. The only people that knew my past in Arizona was my family.

I worked the night shift. It was me and Tracy. God bless his soul. He died a year later. We both sat in a booth watching a shaker screen. Every half hour we had to fill up the bin for the shaker screen. Every time debris got in the way, we had to stop it. One time it was raining, and I had to shut off the power. When I went to turn it back on, I touched the panel box and it threw me ten feet. The Lord was with me then.

It seemed like where ever I went or where ever I worked someone would get me high. I didn't mind because it would relax me. Tracy hooked me up with his wife's girlfriend. Penny was her name. She was beautiful. She was a little taller than me but who cares.

I fell for that girl, but it didn't last. She stole money out of a safe where she worked. The cops couldn't prove it. She did leave town in a hurry. I did get to spend the night with her before she left. She did give me a present before she left. That's something I can't talk about. I never saw her again. It is just as well. My life of crime had ended and hers had just began.

A little while later I was dating the secretary. She was separated from her husband. Her son also worked there. She was older than me, but she was a sweet person. I would get high with her son. I never knew he disliked me for going out with his mother. He ended up setting me up and I got fired. The boss fired me and didn't say why. He just said, we don't need you anymore.

It took me twenty-eight years to figure out why my boss let me go. When I found out, I called my boss and let him know who set me up. My ex-boss apologized to me and said for what it was worth that guy was an alcoholic and was in and out of trouble. He told me, now I am not so easily influenced. We had a good talk and I got that off my chest.

I landed a job at a molding mill. After a year there they made me a super visor. I ran the night shift.

My dad was an antique dealer. He would travel to different states. He had five pickers in different state. When they had a load, my dad would pick it up. Sometimes I would go with him. I learned a lot from my dad. That is why I am so knowledgeable about antiques now. I still buy and sell antiques.

My dad went on a trip with my step mom. That is when I moved out. There was no love on my step mothers' part. You could look at her and see an empty shell, at least I could.

I rented a house behind the apartments where I stayed. Alice was the manager. I went to pay my rent and noticed a woman on the couch. She was Alice's daughter. She was older than me, but I found her attractive. I dated her for a while then she moved in with me. A while later we got married.

Now I had a mother-in-law living with us who was crazy. She wouldn't sleep in her own bed. She had to sleep in the rocking chair every night. It was a trip living with her. I also had an eleven- year-old stepdaughter to raise. I had a readymade family.

My wife was an alcoholic. At first it wasn't bad. She was always in good humor. Being married to her I felt like I was a babysitter. I always did everything for everyone else. My wife wanted to move to Massachusetts to be by her kids. So, I moved the family out there.

We rented an apartment above her daughter's place.

I worked for Consolidated Designs. They made PC boards. The place was crazy. Just about everyone that worked there got high. The boss was a drunk and would be passed out in the hallways at night. It seemed like everyone would cover for him.

I lived twenty-one miles from Boston. The only thing that turned me off about living in the big city was every time I opened the door to my apartment at night, cockroaches would fall on your head. No one really knows about the roaches until they move to a big city. Almost all bigger cities have them After working at that place for seven months the place folded.

My buddy and I got a job at New England Nuclear. We drove twenty miles one way. It was a night job. Chuck and I both worked in different departments. Chuck was a good friend, we did everything together. During the day we worked for a construction firm. We had two bosses, Ozzie and George. We would refurbish old buildings. On the way to work we would stop a few blocks away, there was always a few dealers on the street corner. We would always get three joints. Three for five bucks. Then we would go to the deli and get a nice sandwich. Some of the best I ever tasted. Then we would go to work. We would drive thirty miles to New Hampshire. There was three of us that worked together. No one checked up on us.

Chapter Nineteen

Hit a kid on a bike

While I was living in Massachusetts, I had a variety of jobs. I had a good friend that I hung around with named Chuck I met Chuck when I worked at Consolidated Designs. We made PC boards and different components. More than once a week we had to wash these boards with Trico chlorine, you would get high from the fumes. That was the worst part about that job. Most everyone that worked there did some kind of drugs while they worked. There was a lot of pot smokers and there was a certain few that snorted coke. The boss was a drunk. Almost every night you would find him on the floor somewhere passed out. But everyone covered for him.

I worked there for seven months then the place folded because of the poor quality of work. Chuck knew a lot of people and the next week we started working for a construction firm. My buddy Chuck and his wife would do a little coke occasionally. They would be paranoid when they would go out so they would have me watch their house. I was the only one they trusted because I didn't care for that crap. A little smoke occasionally because it relaxes me. I am a very hyper person.

I moved to this state so my wife could be by her kids. They were grown up and had families of their own. There was no future in this state. Everywhere you went someone would be on a street corner selling drugs. When you got home and opened the door cockroaches would fall on your head. Most of the big cities have them. That is why I never cared for the big city life. You don't know nothing until you travel.

Once in a while Chuck and I would get a night job, so we had extra cash. We got a job at New England Nuclear. One afternoon on our way to work I noticed a kid on a bike coming straight at me. It was a four-lane highway and he was illegally cutting across the freeway from his yard.

He kept coming and getting closer to me. I couldn't believe this kid. He cut right in front of me and I watched him, and his bike slide down my windshield. When the cop arrived on the scene the kid told him that it was his fault. I felt bad for the kid. He was sixteen and was big for his age. His leg was busted up, but he was going to be 0k. My buddy Chuck was so upset that we had to take the night off from work.

All kind of crazy things would happen to me most of my life. I worked there for another few months. I saved enough money so I could move my family back to Arizona. I lived there another year. One of my dads' friends lived a mile down the road. I would help him out occasionally. I would do odd jobs for different people. It wasn't hard to make ends meet. It was good to be back in Arizona. Wide open spaces and no one breathing down your neck.

My dads' friend was dealing with a realtor in Sioux Falls, South Dakota. He bought different types of property cheap. A house and different business. He talked me into buying a house for four thousand dollars. I made payments to my dads' friend. I did this for a year and then I decided to move my family to South Dakota.

My family consisted of my wife, stepdaughter, mother-in-law and our pet cat. I bought a 1959 truck and put a camper on it and we headed out of town.

Chapter Twenty

Ripped off by realtor

We drove for five days and we finally reached South Dakota. When we finally reached our destination, I was in total shock. The house wasn't fit to live in. Inside the house you could see where the water level reached five feet up the wall. My family was just sick. This realtor was selling this property repeatedly. People would expect to move in, and they would be in the same situation I was. I had the fire department burn down the house so he couldn't scam anyone else. I found out that my dads friend made one thousand dollars off me too.

I was scammed by two people. I called that realtor and asked him why he ripped me off. He said his wife was sick and he had a lot of medical bills. He said he would make it up to me, but Lester Larson never did. Things like this keep happening to me, I must be drawn to this kind of people.

We finally found a place to rent in a town twenty miles away. In South Dakota there is no state income tax, so the property is pretty cheap. I did rent with option to buy. The house I was renting, I paid for in one year. It was a two-story house with two and a half lots. I lived two blocks from town. The people were friendly. Some of nicest people you could ever know.

It is who you know, that is how I got a job at a high school. A lady I met went to school with the superintendent. She put in a good word for me and out of the twelve applications I got the job. I worked as a janitor for a few years and when the head janitor didn't work there any more, they gave me that job.

I didn't stay there that long. I was promised a nice raise right away. They lied to me. The secretary told me they put a freeze on the wages. I then turned in my resignation.

I didn't have to work that hard because my house was paid for. I have been blessed all of my life and I didn't stop to smell the roses.

I had a lot of good friends that I hung around with. Two of my buddies and I would put on a hundred or two hundred miles on the weekends looking for old cars. One time I had three old trucks. A Nineteen Fifty-Eight and a Nineteen Fifty-Nine Chevy. I also had a Fifty-Two Ford truck.

South Dakota was full of shelter belts on each farm. They were in a wooded area and could be hard to see. We towed a lot of cars home.

I lived a mile from a lake. We would go night fishing cause the walleyes would come closer to shore. We always got our limit. I was blessed with good friends. You don't find them like that anymore. Now if someone does you a favor, they want to get paid. God has taught me to do things for others. The people who really need it. None of this is possible if you don't have a good heart.

God helped me so much in my life. I think he knew that I wasn't a total waste. He never gave up on me. Good and bad things would happen because of the way that I lived. Most of the bad karma could have been avoided.

You never think about that aspect of life. When you get older you can correct your mistakes. With God in your life every day there is only good things in store for you. I didn't fully live for the Lord. But I always loved him and thanked him for my blessings.

I had five good friends that I hung around with. I had two buddies that would take trips with me looking for old cars. In the farmers shelter belts they were plentiful. We would haul five or so home. It was a good way to spend the day.

The friends that I hung around with were all honest. What is the chance of that? I could count on them and they could count on me. Some of the best times of my life were in South Dakota. I didn't stay there too long after my wife died. I couldn't stay busy enough to make the money that I wanted to make.

I moved back to Wisconsin. I stayed with my brother until I got back on my feet. Three days a week I would do flea markets and the rest of the week I would paint houses. I made good money and I could save being by myself.

After about seven months I was getting a little lonely, so I picked up a paper that advertised dating sites. I wrote to this girl down south. After a month of writing back and forth I drove down to see her.

Chapter Twenty-One

Hired eight times by the same company

I got a job working for a creamery. They gave me a boring job that I didn't like, after I was there for a few hours I told myself I am not going to do this. The guy that trained me wasn't around, so I took off and didn't tell anyone. I heard that the guy looked for me for two hours and he got chewed out for not watching me closer.

A month later they hired me again. I lasted six months this time. I wouldn't take grief from anyone. Back then some people had no class and they would smart off to you. My boss knew that I was a good worker and that is why they hired me so much.

I did get a job at a hospital, I worked there for a year. It was a good place to work. I had to drive twenty-five miles one way. I quit that job and went back to the creamery.

After living in South Dakota for four years, my wife died. I quit my job again. I laid around the house for a year. I didn't feel like doing much. I had my wife insured for $50,000 and my house was paid in full. When you lose a loved one it is hard to keep focused on anything else. You don't want company, you just want to be left alone.

I tried to keep myself occupied. I would go shopping a lot and I even got tired of that. I had a stepdaughter I was putting through college. I put my mother-in-law in a nursing home. She was now, eighty-nine years old. I was not able to take care of her.

My stepdaughter received her bachelor's degree and was working on her masters when she hooked up with this loser. I cut her off from money and I never saw her again. Sometimes you have to practice tough love. She had to learn to take care of herself. She was now twenty-three years old and her boyfriend could help her.

It seemed like one minute I had a family and then just like that, they were all gone.

After laying around for a year I met a woman from Sioux Falls. She had a daycare business and made fifty-five thousand a year. She ended up being nothing but a con artist. She took me for over twenty thousand.

I got a loan to build her a garage and after that I was treated different. I took her and her family to Disney World. She treated me bad all the time I was there. I began to realize what a big mistake I had made.

When you are lonely you have a habit of making mistakes. I let this woman use me and I didn't think that a person could be that cruel or mean. Some people it is their nature. When we would go out to eat, she would make me pay for my own meal. Diane was all about money.

I would watch her on the computer, she was trying to con more guys. The last guy she went with was in construction. He built a slab for her garage and when he was done, she got rid of him. I got out of there. I couldn't take any more abuse.

I was good to her and her two sons. I even paid off a loan for her youngest son. A few weeks later they wanted me to get a loan to buy a new computer. I said no. I got chewed out and screamed at from her and her son that I already helped. Before I left, her older son said, "I wish you could have given me one thousand dollars too."

A snake can lie under any blade of grass. Why me Lord? I said this over and over. I sure made a lot of mistakes and I was always too trusting. I still had my house, so I went back home.

I went back to the creamery again. All together they hired my eight times.

In the town where I lived, I met some of the nicest people. After all that I had been through I didn't think that there were people like that anymore.

Chapter Twenty-Two

Won the lottery

Once I met my new girl, we hit it off. I moved in with her and after a few weeks of getting to know her I got a job at a printing company. I eventually started my own painting and roofing business. I stayed busy night and day.

You learn a lot when you have a business. I painted houses by myself. I did all the roofing alone too. You couldn't find good help. If you hired a big guy he was off that roof every five minutes after the water jug. Some would get paid and buy a bag of dope and then you wouldn't see them again. I learned that the only one that you can trust and that is dependable is yourself.

I didn't mind working by myself because when I got paid the money was all mine. It took me a little longer and I didn't have to be in a hurry. I always worked hard.

After seven months I got married. Once you are married for some time things seem to be a lot different than you expected. I did learn in a hurry; my wife was an alcoholic and eventually I found out she had a gambling problem.

She had an antique mall and I had a booth there. Even though we are married she charged me rent for my booth. Can you believe that? I treated her good and she used me. When you love someone, you do anything for that person. I guess she didn't get that memo.

We lived in an upstairs apartment and at the end of the block was a grocery store. One day on the way to work I stopped at the store and bought a lottery ticket. A few days later I found out that I had won five thousand dollars. That was a wonderful surprise. It didn't take that long before my wife got her hands on it and it was soon gone. I knew this marriage wasn't going anywhere.

I am always making bad choices. I guess sometimes it is better to be lonely. I know that God had his hand in my winning. The Lord giveth and he taketh away. I let the Lord down a lot. He wanted me to make the right choices, but I seem to always get off track.

I was always in a hurry to make things happen. That has always been my downfall. I haven't been hanging around the right crowds either. It is funny how things happen, but it all worked out in the end. I may have avoided all of my troubles by making the right choices.

We were both born on the third of May and we were married on the third of May. Isn't that crazy. It was her idea. I was one year older than her.

I didn't have the perfect marriage and my wife couldn't be trusted. I knew that I was living on borrowed time as she was all about herself. Her girlfriend Anna told me before I married her that she would just cheat on me. She was right. You want to have faith in people and try to see the good in them. It gets harder every day to find a honest and caring spouse. I kept running into users and users. Sometimes you wonder if everyone is like that. That is a sad thought.

God keeps letting me make my mistakes. I guess he thinks that eventually I will figure it out.

Most of her family didn't care for me. None of them would go out of their way to talk to me. They were a different breed of people. Her son was the only one that treated me good. How could anyone be happy in that situation. I've always treated everyone the way I wanted to be treated but there is always someone who thinks they are better than you.

Still to this day I will tell someone off if they have it coming. I have to work on that. I have to stop and think before I speak or respond to something.

Even though I live for God I am not perfect. I am still a sinner, but I try to do my best to please God. Every morning when I awake, I give thanks to our Lord and savior for his blessings and his forgiveness. Most days I praise him all day long. When the Lord is on your mind, your outlook on life is much brighter.

Chapter Twenty-Three

Cops set me up for a bust

I had a few good friends that I hung out with, one of them was my boss at work. I couldn't believe all that went on at work. There were a lot of people who smoked pot at work. You could be high most every day at work. Some of the bosses smoked.

I started a job and I was still in a bad situation. How was this job going to be, I asked myself? They hired illegals all the time. Sometimes I would sit around with my boss doing nothing. I worked there for four years. He knew I was a good worker and he took care of me.

I smoked weed with the rest of them. A lot of us could work better while being stoned. Sometimes you have to go with the flow to fit in.

One day my boss gave me ninety dollars to get him an ounce of weed. I knew where to get it. I used to work with a guy that was a dealer. I went to his house and gave him the money. My buddy and I waited a few days and still didn't hear from him.

A few months ago, my wife and mother-in-law and I went to this trophy hunting lodge. My mother-in-law's boyfriends' sister was with the guy who owned it. They had acres of four-wheel trails. They guy who owned the place drove me around his property. He told me I could get high if I wanted to. So, I pulled out a joint and started to smoke. Then he drove around some. He had a son that was a cop and he lived in the same town as I did.

Anyway, getting back to my buddy and I waiting for the weed. My mother-in-law got a call from someone that was at the game farm and lodge. That cop that lived in the same town where I did was down there drunk and bragging how they were going to set me up for a bust. Someone cared enough about me to tip me off. I won't mention any names. God bless that person. The Lord was looking out for me again.

I knew who set me up, so I called him and told him that cops told me he set me up. I told him that I didn't want that ninety back and just stay away from me. I told him I was going to let everyone know what a snake he was. After that the cops never did come around. I'm sure they never figured out who tipped me off. The cop that was bragging about how they were going to set me up was only twenty-one. You know what they say, don't send a boy to do a man's job.

It wasn't too long after that the wife sold her mall The Lord took care of me, he got me out of that mess. I was making truck payments on her truck.

She didn't want me to own another vehicle. As soon as she got rid of the business then she got rid of me. That shows how I got treated for taking care of her. She also had cancer. I helped her get through that. She gave me fifteen hundred to buy a van to get out of town.

She took her daughter to New York to see 911 and later on that year she took her son to Nashville. It didn't take her long and that money was gone. A fool and their money are soon parted. She wasn't too smart. She had a steady income from the store, and she gambled and drank up the rest.

Now I had a life again. I thank God many times for getting me out of that relationship. The power of prayer helps. You just have to believe. God knows that I love him.

I went to my brother's house until I got back on my feet. Things do have a way of working out. God has never let me down, but I have failed him too many times. I am glad that he is a forgiving God, otherwise there would be no hope.

I was back to working for myself. I was a house painter and I bought and sold antiques. I painted four days a week and every Friday and Saturday I did flea markets. I kept busy. I had a fresh start and I wasn't going to let any distractions get in my way.

Being by myself again, I felt freedom. I had no woman telling me what to do or how to spend my money. When you are in a relationship its fifty-fifty. No one has the right to tell their spouse what to do. That isn't how it works. When you love a person, you will do anything for them. A real man will always put his wife before himself. A woman should be treated like a princess and she shouldn't have any worries.

The more you do for a person, I am talking about doing things of kindness that comes from your heart. You will always be blessed for your kindness. I was raised in a Christian family and I had a wonderful life growing up. There were always functions with relatives.

In the fifties, it was exciting to be a kid. Life was simple back then. No one worried about what someone else was doing. People minded their own business. I saw a lot of bad things growing up, but I never told on anyone.

I was renting a small house from my brother. I was always paid up at least eight months in advance. I always had money in the bank. I was single and I could do that.

I have been back home for a year and a half and the Lord continues to bless me. I am finally living the way I should and no distractions. Now I have finally gotten ahead but there was something missing. A good woman. I was wondering if there was any out there. Now that I was wiser, I was also more cautious.

Chapter Twenty-Four

Wife number five

God always answers my prayers. Once in a while it may take a little longer. I think that he is trying our patience. I have been blessed all my life.

I never took the time to realize it, but God saved me from a lot of sticky situations that I got myself into. I don't think that I would be here now without God in my life. I give my father in heaven praise every day.

My favorite scripture is Deuteronomy-chapter six, verse five. An thou shalt love the Lord thy God with all thine heart and with all they soul and all they might. These are the greatest words to live by. I live by that every day and the Lord has nothing, but goodness planned for me. I can take that to the bank. I can count the many blessings that I have received, and I know that God has more in store for me.

Some days I would buy antiques. I would think about a certain antique and the next day or so I would find it. A lot of times I will be thinking of something or someone and I run into that person. I've had a lot of strange things happen to me over the years or strange occurrences.

One day I was bored so I went out and bought a computer. I was going on different web sites for singles. After a few weeks of learning how to use the computer I began to explore dating sites. This was new to me. But it was kind of exciting.

The first woman I was talking with wasn't that exciting. She didn't have anything going for herself. She was kind of bossy and lived like a bum. I didn't need any more bottom feeders.

The second woman I met online seemed nice. I talked to her for a few days and then we made plans to meet. She lived twenty-five miles away. I could handle that drive. We met on a rainy night. We had a good time and the next day she invited me to her house. A month later I moved in with her. She owned a bar, restaurant and bowling alley business. She also had a mobile home park, a mobile home sales lot and a farm that she rented. She lived in a nice house in the country. I lived with her for eight months before we got married.

There was a lot of responsibilities. I helped her maintain her properties and I had to learn how to fix bowling lane machines when there was a mis-feed or whatever. In the evenings I had to oil the lanes and get them ready for the leagues. On the weekends I had to mow grass at the sales lot and in the park.

I had plenty to do. And every now and then I would bartend. I never cared for that life. She had five or six different bartenders. Almost every one of them was ripping her off. One of the bartenders would steal toilet paper every week. I had to lock everything up. My wife knew these people were ripping her off. I told her to fire them, she told me no they are my friends and that they had to answer to the Lord someday for what they had done. No one respected her. How could they when they would steal every chance they got.

After we closed the bar, we had at least eighteen different customers telling us how the bartenders were ripping us off and giving away drinks and food. It was a no-win situation.

One of the bartenders would take off from the bar with no one to watch it so he could pick up his stepdaughter from school. I would stop at the bar and there wouldn't be a bartender and I would find customers behind the bar pouring themselves free drinks. There were so many people taking advantage of my wife, even some family members.

It is too bad that these people that she knew and served for years would take advantage of her. She always had to borrow money from different people to pay her bills. She was losing hundreds of dollars a week. When she closed the bar, she was owed over eight thousand in bar tabs. She never saw a dime of that money.

One of the bartenders had a friend that drank for free. This was easily a few hundred there and that was only one of the bartenders. The rest were just as bad.

Bar life is no the life for the normal person. My wife's brother and I had to talk my wife into closing down the bar. The bar should have been paid for, but she lost thousands when she closed the place. Now all of these bums had to find someone else to freeload off of.

Her trailer park was about the same situation. A lot of the people that lived there didn't have much ambition and they all ended u owning her money for rent. Money that she never would see.

She had a partner and he was a jerk. He told the banker that when he was done with my wife, she wouldn't have a dime. That sure didn't go over well with me. I called up that drunk and I found out that he was a wife beater. I told him I wanted just five minutes alone with him. He was a wimp that just spouted off at the mouth. He lived in a different town. After that conversation he never came here again. He showed his true colors. He would send his daughter here after that to take care of business. We got a lawyer and finally got out of that mess.

In the end he had to pay all of the extra expenses. I told my wife now we will have a life because we didn't have to cater to no more drunks and bums. I always tell it like it is.

The Lord had better plans for my wife. She didn't know it at the time. It seemed like her world was caving in. She would put her resume in a few places. Some lady called her and told her they had an opening at this newspaper company, and she thought my wife could handle it. My wife went for the interview and got the job.

Chapter Twenty-Five

My wife owns two newspaper companies

I told my wife that she would be rewarded someday for all her hard work. At the time she couldn't see it. I knew God would take care of her.

Wife number five is the best wife I have ever had. She would never complain, she was a good person and she was a lot nicer than my previous wives. She never takes advantage of me. She did more for me than any one of my other wives. The Lord finally gave me a partner that I could trust and grow old with. I was truly blessed.

My wife worked for this newspaper for approximately three years before it was purchased by a new owner. After working under him for approximately two years, he made her his general manager.

When she first started working for the newspaper, she was paid eight dollars an hour. Her new boss knew she was a good worker. The new boss didn't really care too much for the other employees. They were not as ambitious, and some would complain all the time. My wife was given various tasks and she excelled at every one of them. Some of the other workers were jealous and thought that they should have been made the general manager. You can't excel if you are not a good worker. I told me wife that her efforts would pay off. I knew she worked hard, and she would be praised for her efforts.

She got a nice raise with that position. She was always an hour early every day for work. She went that extra mile and her boss noticed her efforts.

I prayed so many times that my wife would have the life she deserved. She learned so much and was so good at every aspect of the business. Her boss knew she was a valuable asset of the company. I couldn't be prouder of her. God gave me a gem when I got her.

She worked as his general manager for another three years. He was then wanting to sell the company so he could move to

Texas to be closer to his daughter. To my wife's surprise he sold her both companies with no money down. She would have to pay him monthly on a land contract for ten years. The newspapers were making money, so it was a no brainer.

She hired new people. One of the gals that worked for her was so lazy that she wouldn't answer the phone even when my wife was busy. My wife cleaned house and now everything is running smoothly. God took care of my wife.

She never expected to own two newspaper companies. The Lord works in mysterious ways. God's love and grace still amazes me. I know that God had a hand in helping my wife. He hasn't let me down yet.

My wife works eleven to twelve hours a day. Even on the weekends she is at home doing work on the computer.

I am retired. I work in the summer part-time painting houses. In the winter I don't do much. I do clean the house and have supper made by the time she gets home. I do whatever errands are needed. That is the least I can do.

My wife has had both businesses for two years now and she plans to retire in six more years. She will then sell both newspapers upon retirement.

We both have been blessed so much and the Lord takes care of us when we follow the right path. I am not perfect by no means and I still have a lot to learn. We all sin, that is a given. It is what we do and how we treat each other in this world that determines our place in heaven.

God has a book on everyone. In each of our books God writes down all of the good deeds that we perform here on earth. It is going to be a sad day if God turns the pages in your book and they are all empty.

That also means that you have an empty heart. All I know is that I love my savior with all my heart, all my might and all my soul. We have been blessed by our Lord and his blessings will never end because I will give God the devotion he deserves.

I am on the right path now. I don't know how I took the wrong turn in life, but I do know I will always live for God and always try to do my best for him. He has done so much for me and he has made my life complete.

I used to have a scrap metal business. One day I picked up this stove from this Christian lady who was blind. I said to her, do you know how everything goes good for awhile and then you have a bad spell for a while. She said, honey that isn't luck you are blessed by the grace of God. I always thought I was lucky. Now I know God had a hand in whatever I do. Thank you, Lord.

When you pray to God every day, what a difference that makes. It is nice to wake up each morning and to appreciate what the Lord has provided. The Lord has taken care of us more than I had ever expected. I have always put others before myself. That was the way I was raised. When you do help someone there is no greater feeling.

I am proud of my wife for going from making eight dollars an hour to owning both newspaper companies. Her hard work paid off. I had faith in her and I knew she would be recognized for all her efforts. No one else did. When you are a good person, good things happen to you. It has always been that way.

God's blessings are for the taking. I praise him, I thank him, and I try to live for him the way he wants me to. That is the hardest part because we are all sinners. We don't want to sin. We are dealt with that reality and we must do our best to please God.

Chapter Twenty-Six

Summing it all up

The Lord has always been my shepherd and most of my life I was one of his flock that went astray. I have always wanted things to happen right away. I never wanted to wait for anything. That kind of logic is what got me in trouble time after time. When you do bad things it only makes matters worse. Nothing good ever came from the bad things that occurred.

When you are young, you are having too much fun with others to realize that what you are doing will have consequences. You do not think of the severity at that time. All you know is that you are having fun. Impressing your friends is what is important to you. I made so many stupid choices. A lot of the time I did things without thinking.

When I robbed that bank, I wasn't thinking of myself. My wife was always telling me how good some of her girlfriends would live. They had this and they had that. I wanted her to have everything she wanted.

My whole life I tried to please everyone else instead of myself. Some people that you helped would always come back for a hand out.

That reminds me of this woman in South Dakota. After my wife died, I paid my brother to remodel my house. This one woman found out that I had a fifty-thousand-dollar life insurance policy on my wife. I could see right through her. She would come over every day for two weeks and sit on my couch watching my brother and I work. I knew she was going to ask me for money, I just didn't know when. She would wear these tiny little dresses, but I was not interested in a con artist.

One day I was at my buddy's house and this woman came looking for me. She finally asked me if I would give her two hundred dollars. I said no and she said why not you can afford it. I chased her away and never saw her again. This world is full of people that try to take away whatever you have. I would always get hooked up with the wrong crowd.

You must be careful what you wish for. After the woman in Sioux Falls that ripped me off, I prayed to God for a poor woman. God gave me a poor woman. She didn't work and didn't have much ambition. I got side tracked again. I had planned to go back to my brothers. I was writing to a woman who was my pen pal and I stopped to see her. It was a two-week delay. This woman was too bossy, so I left.

Even when I escaped from prison, I said Lord don't let me get caught right away. He answered my prayers. He let me go through hell sleeping in rainstorms, covering up with anything to keep the rain off. He let me be sick, I was heaving my guts out and not eating for days, running around in wet clothing, with a rash all over my body and being all scratched up from running through briar patches for a good half hour or so.

Being on the run was no fun. If that wasn't bad enough, I was always looking over my shoulders. God made sure I didn't have a picnic. It was an adventure but not one that I would ever forget. God let me have my adventure but he made sure I never enjoyed myself.

Even when I was locked up in New York, he took care of me. I was on the tenth floor where they kept the escapees and murderers. That was the place to be. The lifers there wanted to do their time without getting into trouble. I don't blame them as their time was long enough and they did not want their stay to get any longer. Some of the lifers that I met were nice people. Any one can go into a rage and kill someone if they are pushed far enough.

Some of these lifers would get me high, they were testing me. And I fit in 0k. Sometimes you must adapt to surroundings that you don't want to just to survive.

I saw a lot of things over the years that I don't like to talk about, and I learned some things that could be fatal to someone if the information got into the wrong hands. I don't want to be responsible for anyone's demise.

Some things are better off left unsaid. There is an old saying, you never let the right hand know what the left hand is doing. You see and hear things that you wish you would have never seen or heard. So mum is the word.

The worse jam I ever got myself into was when I followed some pretty girls that promised me a free meal. They took me to the Alamo Christian Foundation. This was a Christian cult founded in 1969. Sure, I followed these pretty girls to get a free meal and if I hadn't escaped, I don't know if I would have ever made it out. I saw on the news a few years ago that the leader was convicted for molesting young boys. God really save me that time.

People can be convincing, and people want to believe and that is how they get caught up in something that may harm them or do other damage to that person for the rest of their lives.

I have always been a strong-minded person. Now I can tell when I am being conned. You want people around you that are not hateful and full of deceit. Our world is divided now, and I think that is a sign that the world as we know it is in so much turmoil that I am not sure that it can survive.

These are signs that we don't like to see but we must pay attention and live the way God wants us to. I love God and I will never underestimate him. He is real and he gives, and he can also taketh away. He wants us to live for him and show the love and respect that he deserves.

God is worthy of my praise. He is my creator and there will never be anyone as important as him. I give praise to my God day and night. If the world ended tomorrow, I would be ready to meet my maker. Would you?

I am not that same person that I was years ago. I have a purpose now. God gave me life. He taught me what is important. When you can do something for someone else who is in need or has been neglected, it is worth it when you can look them in the face and see they appreciate your help. This is the reward that everyone should be after. God loves us so much when we do that. I'll see God someday and he will know how much he means to me. There is no greater feeling than being Blessed by God.

We must live for God because our number could be called any day. When God wants us to come home, he will bring us to paradise. We will see beauty way beyond our expectations.

Anything can happen to us, good or bad, anytime, anyplace or anywhere. I never expected to rob a bank, hit a kid on a bike, or escape from prison. I never expected to be beaten up by an ex Hells Angel. When I told my classmate after he got hurt in a football game that he would lose his leg...just kidding of course. I never imagined it would come true.

Things happen that we are not supposed to understand. I didn't expect to win the lottery or be married five times. That is why we must be ready to meet God on any given day. We just don't know when our time is up. I don't worry about it, because I love God and God loves me. Every day with the Lord in my heart is a good day.

The most embarrassing moment in my life was when my girls' father...a retired cop... busted me having sex with his daughter. I never went back to his house. How could I? He was a nice guy. That is probably why he didn't tear my head off. I would hang around with him when he worked on his boats. I enjoyed his company. That had something to do with me breaking up with his daughter. I sure could never see her family again. I couldn't look them in the eyes any more. It was stupid on my part, so I just ended the relationship shortly thereafter.

I never expected to match the description of a cop killer. That was the only time that I was glad that I was in jail. That proved my innocence. I had a lot of close calls in life and I think I was being warned to straighten up. God had to be patient with me. He knew how long it would be until I came around to my senses. Now I must show him that I am more deserving of his love.

Every day is an adventure and only good things happen now. We as human beings expect to help each other, and that good feeling is all the reward you need.

I was eighteen years old and I didn't have a dime to my name and my brother kicked and the telephone company entrance would be opened all night so you could use the phone. I thought it would be a good place to sleep. I was wrong, about three o'clock in the morning the police hauled me off to jail.

Just another thing that happened unexpectedly. I did nothing wrong. I got kicked out of the house and tried to get out of the cold to stay warm. Trouble would always seem to follow me and a lot of the time it wasn't my fault.

Even when I was a baby my mother left me in that basket. Now that I think about it, the Lord was watching over me. My great-aunt was the only mom that I knew or ever wanted.

My real mother was an alcoholic and that would have been a real bad life for me. God gave me to a Christian family. It was the best life growing up that anyone could ever ask for. It's too bad my mom died of Parkinson's disease. My brother also died from Parkinson's. We were all exposed to DDT. I had to breath some. I remember the smell as the fogger sprayed the bushes. I often wonder if I got some in my system. There were no health warnings back then. Maybe that would explain why I did such stupid things. Only God knows.

I also remember playing with these sprayers that would spray DDT on the horses to keep off the flies. I probably touched a lot of thing that were poison. I know I played with mercury. Everyone would break thermometers to get the mercury. At least now people know what they are doing. My mom was too busy to watch over me all the time so that gave me the opportunity to get into trouble.

It was a different world back then. Life was simple and people cared about others and a helping hand was always near if you needed one. When you helped someone out you didn't expect to get paid. People weren't all about the money then.

After a bunch of folks were done helping someone, that family would always cook the helpers a nice meal and the fellowship that followed was very rewarding.

A lot of weird things would happen even to my family. When

those deer hunters got killed in Exeland, Wis. only a mile from where my son and his family live. I have a son that lives in Superior, Wis. And that guy who killed those eight deer hunters. His cousin lived next door to my son's place. My son moved away from there.

When I moved to this town it wasn't too long after that a cop killed five high school kids. I was downtown shortly after that happened. I would go at three or four o'clock in the morning to clean our bar. On the morning of the killings a fire truck was parked on the main street. They told us that the cop was on the loose yet and we had to stay locked up in the bar for a while. The cop killed himself, most cowards do. It was sad for a long time.

In nineteen seventy-seven, I was doing time and I had way too much time on my hands so for the heck of it I wrote a letter to Charles Manson's right-hand man, Charles "Tex" Watson. He killed for Manson. I didn't think he would answer me but a few weeks later he did. He was in prison in California and became a Christian. He wrote a book and sent me an autographed copy. The title was "Will You Die For Me." That was the last I ever heard from him. I never wrote back. I just wanted to see if he would answer me and he did.

In my whole life I would never have thought that I would rob a bank. It wasn't planned, it was just a few of us drinking beer at my brother in laws. I guess our liquid courage got the best of us. The next day I said to myself, did I really do that? Things aren't planned. I was at the wrong place, drinking beer and that's all it took.

I don't think that I would be here now if God wasn't watching over me. He helped me get out of a lot of jams. Maybe he thought there was hope for me after all. I praise my Lord every chance I get. If you don't have God in your life you will never have a solid foundation.

A house can not stand if it is divided.

Occasionally you will meet someone, and you will become good friends. I had a good friend like that. We were friends for over fifteen years. He was ten years older than I and we both bought and sold antiques. We had a lot of good times together. One day my vehicle broke down and a week later my buddy Jim walked up to me and told me that he wanted to do something nice for me. I said what is that Jim? He pulled a wad of money out of his pocket that would choke a horse. Jim said I want you to get your vehicle fixed and if you don't take this money, I won't be your friend. I've never had anyone in my whole life do anything like that for me and I probably never will see that again. Jim was a rare friend. He told me one time that he admired me. I said why Jim. He told me that he always wanted to rob a bank but never had the guts. I told him that I wasn't proud of robbing a bank. He was always a good friend. Two years ago, he passed away. I lost my good friend in the Spring and I lost my brother in the Fall. Then on Thanksgiving, I lost my dog. That wasn't a good year.

I know they are all in Heaven looking down on me and occasionally, I sense they are nearby. It is a good feeling and the people close to me I will never forget. Good friends mean more to me than anything else. I've always been blessed that way. Now a true friend is a rare find.

Most of my life I had to fend for myself. I've been on my own since I was eighteen. I had no one that cared that much about me to help me get on my feet. Even when I couldn't find work, I had to do something. You must survive and sometimes you may do things that you don't like. When I was eighteen, I lived with my brother and he could be a pain to live with. In the fall of sixty-nine he threw me out of the house, and I had nowhere to go.

When you are eighteen, you don't know what to do. I had no place to go so I hitchhiked to California. It was getting cold and I needed to be some place where it was warm. Survival at an early age is something that no one should have to think about. I had to grow up in a hurry, keep my ears open and watch my back. I did learn how to survive under any condition.

I learned that I couldn't trust that many people, the world was full of con artists and sometimes I had to think like them to survive.

I did a lot of stupid things in my life and I deeply regret them. I learned from my mistakes. If the Lord hadn't been with me, I may have been locked up for a very long time. God always knew that I loved him. I am sure he wondered when I would come around and give him one hundred percent.

When I was a burglar, I was very lucky. When we got caught, I whispered for my partner to shoot that guy. Of course, I didn't want him to shoot anyone. When you get caught in the act, you say the first thing that comes to your mind without thinking. I wanted my partner to pull the gun on him so we could tie him up so we could get away. God was with us on that day. He knew that we had to be stopped and if he wouldn't have intervened, we would have been sitting for a long time. I've been blessed by God so many times and it finally sunk in that crime wasn't the answer.

It is a known fact that we all belong to Christ and Christ belongs to God. Christ is the light of the world and those that follow him shall never walk in darkness but shall have the light of life as described in St. John chapter eight verse twelve. Living with Christ is a much better place to be. We must strive to be a better person, that is what will keep our existence.

If we treat everyone the way, we want to be treated then there will never be any worries. God wants us to live that way, as a matter of fact he demands it. God had to be praised every day and with that praise will come many blessings. God wants us to have everything that we want but he also wants our complete devotion. It is a no brainer. You give thanks to our creator every day and praise him. You must ask God for forgiveness. If you do that a new world will open to you. You must mean it.

I know I've been blessed repeatedly. When you live for God you have a peaceful feeling. God does answer our prayers. Some get answered right away and some may take a while. And some prayers may be answered in a different way than you expected. Any way it is all good. A day with the Lord our savior is always a blessing. I think back of all the good I could have done early on in life, instead of getting in trouble. I would have been sitting on the top of the world at an earlier age.

Your future is determined by whom you choose to honor. Honor is a seed that will last a life time. Words are the seeds for forgiveness and without faith we have nothing. Life is that simple, Live for God and your life will be blessed by his grace and riches beyond your belief.